Original title:
The Snow's Secret

Copyright © 2024 Swan Charm
All rights reserved.

Author: Olivia Orav
ISBN HARDBACK: 978-9916-79-942-0
ISBN PAPERBACK: 978-9916-79-943-7
ISBN EBOOK: 978-9916-79-944-4

Winter's Unwritten Tales

Snowflakes dance in quiet skies,
Whispers of a world gone cold.
Crisp air wraps like a soft sigh,
Nature's canvas, pure and bold.

Frosted branches hold their breath,
Silence reigns in frosty nights.
Footprints mark the path of death,
Echoes fading, lost in lights.

Fires crackle, warmth inside,
Stories shared in soft embrace.
Time slips by, like a gentle tide,
Memories etched, a fleeting grace.

Moonlight glimmers on the snow,
Dreams drift softly in the dark.
Each heartbeat finds a gentle flow,
As winter sings its quiet lark.

In the stillness lies a spark,
Promises of spring's return.
Hidden tales within the stark,
In the frost, our hearts still yearn.

Crystalline Legends

In the heart of the glade, stars align,
Whispers of ancients, tales intertwine.
Where shadows dance on snow-kissed ground,
A realm of magic in silence found.

Frosted branches sway with grace,
Holding secrets in their embrace.
Echoes of time, both muted and clear,
In crystalline forms, legends appear.

Reflections in a Frozen Pond

Stillness rests on the icy face,
Mirrored stories of a quiet place.
Ripples of thought, trapped beneath glass,
Nature's canvas where moments pass.

With every breath, the world holds tight,
Memories dance in the pale moonlight.
A whisper of dreams, as soft as a sigh,
In frozen depths, they linger and lie.

The Unspoken Beneath

Beneath the snow, life stirs and breathes,
A silent heart that never leaves.
Roots entwined in a secret song,
Hiding where the shadows belong.

In the cold embrace of winter's reign,
Stories unfold in quiet vein.
Whispers of hope beneath the frost,
In every silence, not all is lost.

Hushed Beneath a Canopy of White

A blanket deep, the world in trance,
Nature's breath in a gentle dance.
Snowflakes fall like whispered dreams,
Clad in white, the landscape gleams.

Time slows down in the winter air,
Each flake a tale with stories to share.
Beneath the stillness, life softly glows,
Hushed beneath where the soft wind blows.

The Quiet Within the Storm

The wind howls wild and free,
Clouds churn in a dark ballet.
Yet within the tempest's heart,
A silent place finds its way.

Raindrops beat a steady drum,
Nature's pulse in restless beat.
Calm exists in every drop,
Whispers soft in chaos' heat.

Lightning dances, flashes bright,
Illuminating chaos, brief.
Stillness hangs in sudden light,
A fleeting moment, sweet relief.

Roots hold strong beneath the ground,
Where peace and strength intertwine.
In the storm, the quiet found,
Echoes of the grand design.

As chaos rages, hearts grow clear,
Listen close, the truth resounds.
In the storm, a voice to hear,
The quiet place where hope abounds.

Ledger of the Frozen

In the mirror of the lake,
Ice reflects the silent trees.
Frozen whispers, stories lost,
Nature's hush on winter's knees.

Each flake writes a tale untold,
Patterns dance upon the white.
A ledger bound by frost and cold,
Moments captured, pure, and bright.

Footprints mark the icy ground,
Silent stories left to freeze.
Every echo, every sound,
Memories hang like frozen leaves.

Beneath the surface, life still stirs,
Awake in slumber, hidden deep.
Ledger kept with quiet purrs,
Secrets kept while world's asleep.

Time stands still in snowy halls,
Nature's breath held in soft snow.
Within this world where silence calls,
Life persists, unseen, aglow.

Chasing Flurries

Snowflakes whirl in winter's dance,
Caught in laughter, light as air.
Chasing dreams with every chance,
A fleeting glimpse, a whispered prayer.

Children run through fields of white,
Gleeful shouts and brightened eyes.
Every flurry, pure delight,
Moments glisten like the skies.

Windswept trails lead hearts away,
Down the paths where spirits play.
Chasing flurries, lost in time,
Every heartbeat, every rhyme.

Night descends, the world aglow,
Blanketed in frosty calm.
Dreams take flight in flakes that flow,
Cradled in the night's sweet psalm.

In the stillness, echoes fade,
Memories dance in soft embrace.
Chasing flurries, joys remade,
Life's a race, yet slow the pace.

A Veil of Ice

A veil of ice, clear and cold,
Cloaks the world in silver light.
Nature's canvas, wondrous, bold,
Framed by dusk, just out of sight.

Branches draped in crystal lace,
Sparkle gently, catch the eye.
Each one holds a frozen trace,
Of winter's breath, a whispered sigh.

In the quiet, shadows play,
Figures dance beneath the moon.
A veil of dreams guides the way,
Hushed beneath the night's soft tune.

Every step, a careful grace,
Cracks beneath the frozen spell.
Glimmers flicker, fleeting chase,
A tale that time dared not to tell.

As dawn arrives, the veil will fade,
A world reborn in morning's kiss.
Yet in the heart, the memories stayed,
Of winter's breath and icy bliss.

Traces of Frosty Footsteps

In the silent morning light,
Footsteps whisper, soft and slight,
Each print a story left behind,
Nature's secrets intertwined.

Shadows dance upon the snow,
Where the chilly breezes blow,
Tracks that lead to nowhere clear,
Memories of winter near.

With each step, a tale unfolds,
Frosted paths the heart beholds,
A journey through the crystal haze,
Lost in winter's frozen maze.

Nature's breath, a frosty sigh,
Underneath the blushing sky,
Crisp and cold, the world confined,
Traces of what we leave behind.

In the dusk, the shadows play,
As daylight starts to fade away,
The frosted prints fade with the night,
Whispers lost in purest white.

The Chamomile and the Snowflake

Amidst the swirl of winter's chill,
A chamomile beneath the hill,
Frosty flakes descend with grace,
Kissing petals' soft embrace.

Every flake a dancer bright,
Spinning down in pure delight,
While the flowers, brave and bold,
Hold their warmth against the cold.

Gentle whispers in the air,
Of blooms that thrive with tender care,
Snowflakes twirl in soft ballet,
Nature's art on display.

A harmony that speaks of peace,
Where winter's grasp finds sweet release,
Chamomile and snow unite,
Creating wonders, pure and white.

Each serenity interlaced,
In this tranquil, frosty space,
Where the cold and warm collide,
In the heart of winter, side by side.

Ethereal Shroud of White

A blanket soft, an ethereal shroud,
Covers all beneath the cloud,
Glistening in the morning dawn,
Where the world is reborn and drawn.

Whispers float on frosty air,
Voices lost, but still they care,
As nature dons her winter dress,
In the silence, purest bliss.

Crystals form on every branch,
In the quiet, still we prance,
Through the woods, a dreamlike state,
Curving paths that lead to fate.

Footsteps crunch on snowy ground,
Where every moment can be found,
In this realm of white and light,
Hope and peace in winter's sight.

The day unfolds in softest hues,
As twilight bathes in twilight's cues,
An ethereal dance that takes its flight,
In the beauty of the night.

In the Heart of the Chill

In the heart of winter's chill,
The world lies quiet, calm and still,
Breath of frost upon the air,
Transforming all with tender care.

Whispers weave through branches bare,
Touched by magic everywhere,
Time stands still, a frozen love,
Gift of beauty from above.

The chill brings forth a wondrous sight,
As stars emerge in velvet night,
Moonlight paints the fields so bright,
While dreams take flight in pure delight.

Snowflakes waltz to nature's song,
In this stillness, we belong,
Wrapped in warmth, we hold each other,
Hearts aglow, like sister, brother.

When the dawn begins to break,
And shadows dance upon the lake,
In the heart, the chill we find,
Brings us closer, intertwined.

Echoes of the Frosted Landscape

In silence deep, the whispers flow,
Beneath the trees, where cold winds blow.
Each crystal flake, a tale retold,
Of winter nights, both fierce and bold.

Footprints mark the ways we tread,
In frozen dreams, where thoughts are led.
The world is hushed, a canvas white,
As nature sleeps through silvered night.

A glimmer shines in morning's grace,
Reflecting light on winter's face.
Where shadows dance in pale moon's glow,
The echoes call, past paths we know.

With every gust, the trees respond,
Their branches bare, a silken bond.
In frosty air, the breath we take,
Is woven tight, in memory's wake.

So let us walk through this terrain,
Where echoes linger, stark yet plain.
In every flake, a story spun,
Of frost and time, forever one.

Tranquil Spirits of the Snow

In the stillness of a world so bright,
Whispers soften the edge of night.
Gentle flakes, like whispers fall,
Embracing the earth, a tender shawl.

Each breath we take, a moment close,
As moonlight drapes in quiet prose.
The spirits whisper through the frost,
In every drift, we find what's lost.

Time slows down in this snowy glow,
Where peace resides, as rivers flow.
Nature's lullaby in twilight's reign,
Concealing joy, but never pain.

Every step is soft and slow,
As we travel where wild things grow.
The tranquil spirits guide our way,
Through winter's heart, to break of day.

In twilight's clutch, the stars ignite,
Beneath their watch, the world feels right.
With frosty breath, we join the dance,
In this serene, enchanting trance.

Glimmers in the Cold

The sun peeks through a frosty veil,
A hint of warmth in winter's tale.
Glimmers spark on snow's bright crest,
Awakening dreams from nature's rest.

Icicles hang like jewels of glass,
In the silent woods where shadows pass.
Each glimmer states, in shimmering lows,
That beauty lies where the cold wind blows.

We wander paths, both lost and found,
In frosted realms where peace is crowned.
The echo of laughter, faint yet bold,
Carried high on breezes cold.

Through whispering pines, the story flies,
As every flake tells of the skies.
With each soft step on powdered ground,
The glimmers in the cold abound.

In stillness, there's magic all around,
In every corner, wonder's found.
A tapestry woven in white and gold,
Echoing life in the heart of cold.

Secrets Carried on the Wind

The wind howls softly, secrets spread,
Through branches bare, and pathways tread.
Carried whispers through the night,
As shadows gather, dimmed by light.

In winter's grip, the stories flow,
From mountain tops and valleys low.
Every gust brings tales of old,
Of love and loss, both brave and bold.

With every chill, the heartbeats race,
In the twilight, we find our place.
The whispers tell, of dreams once bright,
Now wrapped in snow, hidden from sight.

The trees listen with patient ears,
As winter holds, the heart's true fears.
Yet hope is carried, on the breeze,
A promise made, to seek and seize.

So let the wind weave through our days,
A gentle touch, a tender gaze.
For in its breath, our secrets blend,
In winter's arms, where pathways wend.

Unraveled by Ice

Beneath the frost, the world does sleep,
Whispers of winter secrets deep.
Branches bend, adorned with white,
Nature holds her breath at night.

Crystal shards catch morning's glow,
Silent tales that only snow can show.
Footsteps echo, soft and light,
In the stillness, hearts take flight.

Secrets in the Snowflakes

Each flake a whisper, pure and bright,
Stories woven in soft white light.
Dancing gently, they grace the ground,
In their descent, magic is found.

Children's laughter fills the air,
Creating castles with love and care.
Underneath the pale moon's glow,
Secrets hidden in freshly fallen snow.

The Quietive Dance of Flurries

Softly swaying, they swirl around,
In silence, joy and peace abound.
A gentle waltz on winter's breath,
Embracing life, defying death.

Spinning dreams in the chilly breeze,
Every flurry aims to please.
Twirling softly, they paint the night,
A canvas of white, pure delight.

Soft Murmurs of Winter

In the hush of the falling snow,
Nature whispers secrets low.
Frosty air carries tales untold,
Of silent nights and days of old.

Boughs bow down with a frozen grace,
As winter weaves her soft embrace.
Heartbeats match the stillness here,
In soft murmurs, winter's near.

Mysteries in the Blizzards' Embrace

Snow whispers softly in the night,
Carrying secrets, pure and white.
Haunting figures dance in frost,
In the blizzards, all seems lost.

Footprints vanish in the storm,
Nature's chill begins to warm.
Stories hidden in the haze,
Waiting for the light's warm gaze.

Branches bow with weighty snow,
Silent tales that none may know.
The howling winds, a haunting sound,
In every flake, lost dreams are found.

Shadows merge with the drifts,
Time stands still as the world shifts.
In the heart of winter's grip,
Lies the truth in nature's script.

Embrace the cold, embrace the night,
In the darkness, find your light.
For within the blizzard's hold,
Live the mysteries of the bold.

Lantern of the Winter Night

A lantern glows through falling snow,
Casting warmth with golden glow.
It dances bright against the dark,
Guiding travelers, leaving a mark.

Chill whispers through the frozen air,
While shadows creep with quiet care.
The flickering flame, a beacon bright,
Holds the secrets of the night.

Stars twinkle in the icy dome,
Reminding hearts that they are home.
Each flicker tells a tale of old,
Of journeys brave and spirits bold.

As snowflakes drift, the world is still,
The lantern's glow, a gentle thrill.
In the embrace of winter's kiss,
Find the warmth of nightly bliss.

Through the dark and silent trees,
The lantern beckons with sweet ease.
In its light, the winter's fear,
Turns to joy as it draws near.

Frosty Secrets Underneath

Beneath the snow, a world sleeps tight,
Wrapped in blankets of pure white.
The earth holds tales of warmth and grace,
In its cold depths, a hidden place.

Whispers of life beneath the frost,
Where time is still, and moments lost.
Roots intertwine in a frozen dance,
In darkness lies a silent chance.

Icicles hang like crystal tears,
Guarding the past through all the years.
Quiet stories carved in ice,
Each one a treasure, worth the price.

When spring arrives, the thaw will bring,
Awakening life, a vibrant spring.
Yet in the chill, the secrets lay,
Awaiting warmth to light the way.

So tread softly on the snow's embrace,
There lie the dreams in nature's grace.
For every frost has its own tale,
Of life's persistence, strong and frail.

The Mirage of White

A field of white, a dream so clear,
The world transformed, with nothing near.
A mirage dances in the bright,
Whispers of beauty in the light.

The horizon blurs, a phantom sight,
Cotton clouds in the endless flight.
Footsteps fade on the snowy crest,
Lost in dreams where hearts find rest.

As shadows stretch in twilight's glow,
The shimmering white begins to flow.
In the quiet, a magic plays,
Creating wonders in soft arrays.

Yet beneath the veil of winter's charm,
Lies the promise of spring's warm balm.
For every mirage, fleeting and bright,
Holds a truth in the heart's pure light.

So wander through this frosty scene,
Where whispers dance and spirits glean.
Embrace the magic, the white delight,
And find your dreams in the starry night.

Under a Shroud of Frost

Morning glimmers with icy grace,
Nature's breath wears a frosty face.
Trees adorned in silver lace,
Whispers of winter, a soft embrace.

Footsteps crunch on frozen ground,
Silence echoes, a haunting sound.
Windows gleam, the world unbound,
In the stillness, peace is found.

Stars twinkle in the crisp night air,
Moonlight dances without a care.
Chill envelops, a gentle snare,
Under a shroud, the earth lays bare.

Fire crackles, warmth draws near,
In this cocoon, we shed our fear.
Time stands still, the end is clear,
Under frost's watch, we persevere.

Hidden Threads of Chill

Veils of snow like whispers fall,
Nature's quiet, a chilling call.
Breath of winter, a silent thrall,
Entwined in beauty, we stand tall.

Frosted leaves and barren trees,
Softly swaying in the breeze.
Buried secrets beneath the freeze,
In the stillness, the heart finds ease.

Icicles drip from rooftops high,
Reflecting echoes of the sky.
Beneath the chill, dreams slip by,
Hidden threads weave as time flies.

Each breath a puff of fleeting smoke,
In winter's grasp, we softly choke.
Yet in this peace, a spark awoke,
Hope hidden deep, like a gentle cloak.

The Silent Tapestry

Woven clouds in shades of grey,
Unfurl their whispers, come what may.
On the horizon, night holds sway,
In this tapestry, shadows play.

Gentle snowflakes drift and sway,
Painting silence, a soft ballet.
Each moment held in dim display,
A quiet song that won't decay.

Footprints lead on paths unknown,
Underneath the stars, we have grown.
Every thread, a tale we've sown,
In the quiet, our hearts have flown.

Beneath the arch of silver light,
Secrets whispered through the night.
In winter's grasp, the world feels right,
A silent tapestry in sight.

Shadows in the Blizzard

Whirling winds and dancing flurries,
The stormy night, it flares and hurries.
In the chaos, no one worries,
For warmth resides in hidden furries.

Shadows cast by flickering flame,
Chilling whispers, they call our name.
Cloaked in snow, the world feels tame,
Yet in this wild, we play the game.

Snowdrifts rise like silent waves,
Buried dreams in frosty graves.
In the blizzard, the spirit braves,
Through the shadows, the heart enslaves.

Cold embraces, a gripping fate,
Yet we stand tall, never late.
In winter's arms, we celebrate,
The shadows in the blizzard's weight.

Whispers of Winter's Veil

Gentle winds begin to sigh,
As snowflakes dance from the sky.
Trees stand tall, their branches bare,
Winter whispers, pure and rare.

Footprints fade upon the ground,
In silence, beauty can be found.
The world wrapped in a glistening shroud,
Nature's secrets speak aloud.

Fires crackle, warmth inside,
While outside, the cold does abide.
Hot cocoa steams in the night,
Winter's magic shines so bright.

Under stars that shimmer clear,
Memories made from far and near.
With every breath, the chill we taste,
In winter's hold, we are embraced.

As days grow short, the nights extend,
In the stillness, hearts can mend.
Whispers of a world anew,
In winter's veil, there's hope for you.

Crystal Silence

In the stillness of the night,
Moonlight casts a silver light.
Snowflakes fall with gentle grace,
Quiet dreams in this safe space.

The world transforms, so pure and bright,
Each breath fogs in the cool night.
Frozen whispers fill the air,
Echoes soft, beyond compare.

Crystals gleam on branches high,
A diamond dance against the sky.
Empty streets, the time stands still,
In this calm, the heart can fill.

Winter's hush, a soothing balm,
Embracing all with tranquil calm.
In crystal silence, peace we find,
A gentle balm for restless minds.

With every flake, a story's spun,
In the quiet, we become one.
Listen close, let worries fade,
In the silence, dreams are made.

Frosted Dreams Beneath

Underneath the frosty ground,
Whispers of spring can be found.
Seeds are dreaming, deep in sleep,
Waiting for the time to leap.

Layers thick of winter's white,
Hold the promise of the light.
Nature pauses, holds its breath,
In this frost, there's life, not death.

Colors waiting, soft and mild,
Springtime's kiss will be so wild.
But for now, the world is still,
In frosted dreams, we find our will.

Underneath, the earth prepares,
For vibrant blooms, the joy it shares.
In silence, life is gathering strength,
For the season's dance at length.

Dreams are woven, pure and bright,
Beneath the snow, hidden from sight.
Wait with patience, spring will show,
The frosted dreams that lie below.

Veiled in White

A blanket soft, a gentle white,
Covers all in a tender light.
Houses cozy, fires aglow,
Veiled in white, the world moves slow.

The quiet hour, the magic hour,
Winter's breath, a fleeting power.
In this stillness, hearts align,
Veiled in white, the world divine.

Children laughing, spirits high,
Snowmen stand under the sky.
Joy and wonder fill the air,
Veils of snow, beyond compare.

Each flake unique, a fleeting joy,
Crafted wonders, none can destroy.
In every turn, the beauty flows,
Veiled in white, the cold wind blows.

As evening falls, the stars awake,
Winter's chill the darkness makes.
In silent nights, dreams take flight,
For all is calm, veiled in white.

Quietude in Crystal

In the hush of dawn's embrace,
Whispers dance on silver lace.
Softly shines the morning light,
Bathe the world in pure delight.

Glistening fields of frozen dew,
Nature's breath, so fresh and new.
Every crystal, every gleam,
Threads together like a dream.

Beneath the boughs, a calm retreat,
Where the heart and soul can meet.
Silence sings in every nook,
In this place, all worries shook.

Time stands still, as moments freeze,
Wrapped in warmth of winter's please.
A tranquil pause in life's parade,
In crystal quiet, dreams are laid.

Here in quietude, we find,
Echoes of a gentle mind.
In each flake, a story spins,
As warmth from within begins.

The Silent Canvas

In twilight's glow, the colors blend,
A canvas waits, where brush strokes end.
Each shade whispers of tales unsaid,
In silent hues, dreams are fed.

Soft whispers of the evening breeze,
Catch the whispers from the trees.
A palette drawn from twilight's grace,
Capturing time in sacred space.

Stars above begin to blink,
Ink spills softly, as thoughts sink.
Every splash of midnight blue,
A heartbeat captured, quiet too.

In strokes of white, the moonlight gleams,
Painting softly through our dreams.
The silent canvas calls to heart,
In art, we find where feelings start.

Here where shadows gently play,
Art creates its own ballet.
With every layer, life unfurls,
In silent beauty, magic swirls.

Secrets of the Winter Chill

Beneath the frost, the secrets lie,
In silent whispers from the sky.
Each breath of winter tells a tale,
Of ghostly winds that softly wail.

Icicles hang like glassy dreams,
Reflecting light in fragile beams.
The world, a tapestry of white,
Stitched with shadows deep in night.

Footsteps crunch upon the ground,
Echoing stories all around.
Frozen lakes, they hold their voice,
In chilling depths, we make our choice.

Secrets sleep in blankets cold,
In winter's arms, the world feels bold.
With every flake, a secret spins,
Each whisper holds where truth begins.

Beneath the stars, the night unfolds,
In winter's chill, warm hearts feel gold.
The beauty lies in quiet pause,
In frozen breaths, we find our cause.

Veils of Frosted Dreams

A shroud of frost on night's delight,
Veils the world in silver light.
Softly sighs the winter air,
Whispers lost, yet always there.

Through the mist, a figure glows,
Wrapped in dreams that winter sows.
With every step, enfolded grace,
In frosted realms of time and space.

Sparkling stars like jewels twine,
In the fabric of the divine.
Each breath, a puff of crystal air,
Concealing dreams beyond compare.

Quiet laughter dances near,
In the veils, it draws us near.
We wander through this sacred night,
With hearts aglow, in pure delight.

In soft embrace of dreams untold,
Veils of frost, a treasure gold.
Wrapped in warmth, our spirits soar,
In frosted dreams, we seek for more.

Winter's Hidden Memoir

In silence falls the crystal snow,
A blanket soft, a whispered glow.
Each flake a tale from skies above,
Winter's breath, a frozen love.

Beneath the chill, the world lies still,
Magic stirs against its will.
Footprints mark where dreams have danced,
In twilight's grip, we hold our chance.

The darkened trees in white adorned,
Nature's canvas, beauty born.
In every shade, a story sewn,
Winter reveals what had been known.

With every gust, the secrets lost,
Held tight in frost, we pay the cost.
Yet in the cold, warmth's ember glows,
Love remains where the winter blows.

So linger here in timeless grace,
Embrace the chill, the soft embrace.
For in this season, memories thrive,
A hidden memoir comes alive.

Crystal Memories

Across the field, the ice does gleam,
A world transformed, a fractured dream.
Each branch adorned with diamond light,
We chase the day, we seek the night.

Frozen laughter, echoes clear,
Moments grasped, yet disappear.
In every glint, a memory holds,
Whispers of warmth the winter folds.

As stars twinkle in the frozen air,
We weave our dreams without a care.
Each flake that falls, a wish reborn,
In crystal memories, love is sworn.

Through sighs of wind, a soft caress,
Holding tight to happiness.
In winter's heart, we find our way,
As memories shimmer, night and day.

So let us dance on frozen ground,
In fleeting moments, joy is found.
With every chill that graces skin,
Crystal memories begin to spin.

The Tapestry of Frost

Each morning paints a wondrous scene,
A tapestry of white and green.
Threads of frost weave through the air,
A story spun with utmost care.

Beneath the quilt of snow so deep,
Nature whispers, secrets keep.
Every twig, a delicate art,
A frozen verse that warms the heart.

The sun will rise and melt away,
Yet in our hearts, these moments stay.
With every shimmer, every hue,
The tapestry reveals what's true.

In winter's grasp, we find our muse,
A dance of light, we cannot lose.
As frost unfurls its gentle grace,
We embrace this sacred space.

So hold the beauty, let it flow,
In every corner, life will grow.
Through icy whispers, love will prove,
The tapestry of frost will move.

Shrouded in White

A veil of silence drapes the night,
Wrapped in warmth, shrouded in white.
Footsteps quiet on the ground,
In this stillness, peace is found.

The world transformed, each edge defined,
In snowflakes, stories intertwine.
A shimmer dances on the stream,
As winter casts its gentle dream.

The moonlight bathes the fields in glow,
As darkness meets the purest snow.
Each breath a mist, a moment shared,
In winter's arms, we're unprepared.

Yet here, within this frozen bliss,
We find the warmth of every kiss.
In soft embrace, let time stand still,
For in this magic, hearts we fill.

So linger long beneath the sky,
Take in the beauty, let it lie.
For shrouded in white, we find our grace,
In every breath, a sweet embrace.

Whispers of the Frozen Realm

In twilight hush, the shadows tease,
Whispers dance upon the breeze.
Icicles glisten, sharp and bright,
Holding secrets of the night.

Beneath the cloak of snowy white,
Dreams emerge in soft moonlight.
Footprints trace the paths once trod,
Echoes of the earth and God.

Silent woods hold tales untold,
In every flake, a world of gold.
Branches sway in quiet grace,
Nature's arms, a warm embrace.

Frost-kissed air, a crystal spell,
Nature whispers, all is well.
In this realm where time stands still,
Hearts ignite with winter's thrill.

From icy streams, the sighs arise,
Mirrored dreams in frozen skies.
In every hush, a story swells,
Of whispered secrets, winter tells.

Secrets in the Winter Light

Morning breaks with gilded sight,
Softly glows the winter light.
Shadows linger, secrets share,
A silent hush hangs in the air.

Frosted window tales unfold,
Silent secrets, shyly told.
In the glow of candles near,
Whispers float, so sweet and clear.

Drifting snow, a gentle veil,
Echoes faint of every trail.
Within this calm, a pulse beats true,
Winter's charm invites the new.

Glistening flakes, a tapestry,
Woven dreams of what can be.
In the crispness lies delight,
Holding magic, pure and bright.

Through the pines, the breezes rush,
In their cadence, voices hush.
Each glow a memory held tight,
In the secrets of winter light.

The Covert Grace of Frost

Underneath a blanket cold,
Whispers of the frost unfold.
Glistening like diamonds rare,
Nature breathes in silent prayer.

Branches wear a crystal crown,
As Winter weaves her soft, down gown.
In every nook, a spark of grace,
A quiet dance in time and space.

Frozen streams like silver lace,
Gather stories, hold their place.
In the hush, old echoes speak,
Murmured songs for hearts that seek.

Frosty breath upon the glass,
Moments captive as they pass.
The world transformed, keen eyes behold,
Covert grace in winter's fold.

Here in peace, the wild things play,
In the light of fading day.
The covert grace, a fleeting sight,
Embraced within the winter's night.

Illuminated By Winter's Touch

A dawn awash in icy hue,
World transformed by morning dew.
Each branch draped in shimmering white,
Illuminated by winter's light.

Whispers linger in the frost,
Memories of warmth embossed.
Through the pines, a gentle sigh,
Nature speaks as time goes by.

Chill in air, so crisp and bright,
Drawing hearts to stay the night.
Under stars, the silence glows,
Each moment whispers, softly flows.

Amidst the snowflakes' gentle fall,
Winter's rhythm, a sacred call.
Hearts entwined in purest grace,
Illuminated by this place.

As night descends, the world stands still,
In the quiet, there is thrill.
Embrace the touch, the beauty found,
In winter's heart, love is unbound.

Enchanted by Frost

Morning light whispers soft,
Blankets of frost unfurl.
Nature's breath, crisp and clear,
Awakens a frozen world.

Trees wear gowns of silver lace,
While shadows dance and play.
A hush falls on the landscape,
In this magical, cold sway.

Footprints crunch on icy trails,
Each step a fleeting echo.
Stars still twinkle from above,
In the silent, frosty meadow.

As the sun begins to rise,
Colors blend, a gentle kiss.
Transforming all that is plain,
Into a realm of pure bliss.

Evening brings a gentle chill,
With whispers of the night.
Enchanted by winter's touch,
We find warmth in frosty light.

Whirling Dervishes of Winter

Snowflakes swirl in twilight's glow,
A dance of joy, a silent show.
Spinning softly, hearts embrace,
In the slippery, wintry space.

Wind chimes sing from high above,
While branches sway like palms in love.
Each gust spins stories of the past,
In fleeting moments that hold fast.

Twilight drapes the world in grace,
As silence marks this icy place.
The dervishes of winter whirl,
In a dance of diamonds, twirl.

Chill embraces every soul,
In this serene, enchanted role.
With laughter lingering in the air,
We swirl with joy, devoid of care.

As the stars begin to gleam,
And dreams take flight like snowflakes seem,
We find ourselves in winter's hold,
As dervishes of frost unfold.

A Palette of Pure White

Under skies of muted gray,
A canvas fresh in every way.
Brush strokes glisten, soft and bright,
Nature's art in purest white.

Fields are blanketed so deep,
Where dreams of warmth and spring can creep.
Every edge and curve defined,
In the beauty, peace we find.

Icicles hang from eaves adorned,
Creating sculptures, beauty formed.
With every flake, a tale to share,
As winter paints with utmost care.

Light reflects on snowy plains,
Whispers carried on chilly veins.
Time seems still, as if to wait,
For spring's embrace, a love innate.

Yet here we stand, in winter's grasp,
Holding memories, soft as a clasp.
A palette pure, so rich and grand,
In every corner of this land.

Frost-kissed Reveries

In the stillness of the dawn,
Frost-kissed dreams are gently drawn.
Each breath a cloud, a whispered wish,
In this fleeting, cold abyss.

Morning glories, touched by frost,
Reveal the warmth that they have lost.
Yet beauty lingers, soft and near,
In every frozen moment here.

Silence wraps the world in peace,
As nature's whispers start to cease.
Thoughts take flight on winter's breeze,
In reveries, our hearts find ease.

Glancing at the distant snow,
We breathe in deep; let worries go.
For in this space of winter's grace,
Our souls find solace, their rightful place.

So let us wander, hand in hand,
Through this enchanted, frosty land.
Where dreams are spun, and hearts hold tight,
To frost-kissed reveries, pure and bright.

Hidden Echoes of Ice

In silence deep, the whispers flow,
The shivering winds, they start to blow.
Beneath the frost, where secrets lie,
Time stands still as shadows sigh.

Frozen lakes hold tales untold,
Worn by ages, bitter and bold.
Glaciers hum in a haunting tune,
Beneath the watch of a silent moon.

Glimmers dance on a crystal shore,
Each echo calls for one yearning more.
In this vastness, hearts entwine,
Wrapped in warmth, though cold they pine.

Nature's breath in a chilling breeze,
Whispers, like ghosts, in ancient trees.
The world is hushed, its beauty vast,
All speak softly of a distant past.

Yet in this place where spirits roam,
Cold as ice, yet feels like home.
Hearts ignite with a warming flare,
Hidden echoes linger in the air.

Mystic Feathers of the North

In twilight skies where shadows glide,
Soft feathers fall by winter's side.
Each drift a whisper, gentle and slow,
Mysterious wonders of the snow.

Beneath the stars that flicker bright,
Dreams take flight in the deep of night.
The auroras dance with painted light,
Embracing hearts in pure delight.

Echo of wings in the frosty air,
Nature's magic, beyond compare.
A call resounds through the silent pines,
Where spirits gather, and love aligns.

The wind sings songs of wanderers lost,
In search of warmth, at any cost.
Each feather tells of journeys made,
In the arms of night, their tales cascade.

With every flutter, hope ignites,
In the chilly glow of starry nights.
Mystic feathers, soft and free,
Guide the way for those who see.

Lullaby of the Frozen World

Hush now, dear, and close your eyes,
The snowflakes whisper soothing lies.
The moonlight bathes the earth in peace,
As winter's song begins to cease.

Under blankets of soft, white cotton,
Dreams awaken, though daylight's forgotten.
The frozen trees stand still and tall,
Guardians of secrets, they hear it all.

In the hush of night, the world sleeps tight,
While stars adorn the blanket of night.
Each twinkle sings a gentle tune,
Beneath the glow of a silver moon.

Snow drifts softly on the ground,
In this embrace, enchantment found.
A lullaby sung by nature's breath,
In the arms of winter, life finds rest.

Let the cold winds cradle your dreams,
In quiet moments, hear the moonbeams.
For in this frozen, serene world,
A lullaby of love is unfurled.

Shadows Beneath the Snowfall

Gray clouds weave a fabric dense,
As shadows dance, in silence immense.
Beneath the snow, stories sleep,
In gentle mounds, their secrets keep.

The world is hushed; a tranquil sigh,
As flakes fall softly from the sky.
Each flurry whispers of days gone by,
In the stillness, memories lie.

Footprints fade in the frosty air,
Lost in time, they vanish bare.
But each shadow casts a soft trace,
Of laughter shared in this quiet place.

With twilight's brush, the earth transforms,
As night blankets shapes and forms.
Each flake a thread in the tapestry,
Binding us to the mystery.

Under the glow of a pale streetlight,
Shadows lurk, longing for flight.
And in their dance, we find our way,
Through the white veil of the coming day.

The Fine Line of Chill

In twilight's grace, the cold air bites,
Stars above, like glimmering lights.
Each breath a cloud, a fleeting sign,
We walk the edge, the fine line of chill.

Soft whispers dance through icy trees,
Branches sway with effortless ease.
Footsteps crunch on the frosty ground,
Finding warmth where solace is found.

Silent nights cloak the world in peace,
As the winter's heart begins to cease.
Beauty lies in the stillness profound,
In this embrace, we are tightly bound.

The fire crackles within our souls,
Gathered close, we feel the warmth rolls.
Outside, the frost wraps up the night,
Inside, our hearts are burning bright.

With a cup of joy, we sip the frost,
In this moment, we count the cost.
Cherishing the warmth, we linger still,
Forever held by the fine line of chill.

Dance of the Winter Spirits

In the hush of night, spirits glide,
Through gentle snow, they twist and slide.
With laughter carried on the breeze,
They weave through dreams, like whispers, they tease.

Moonlight glimmers on frozen streams,
Casting shadows on our winter dreams.
With each flurry, a graceful spin,
The dance begins, it draws us in.

Among the pines, their laughter rings,
Echoing softly, the joy it brings.
As they twirl in the silver light,
We watch in awe, this magic sight.

Every snowflake, a note in flight,
Plays a tune that feels just right.
In this symphony, the soul takes wing,
To the beat of winter spirits singing.

As dawn arrives, the dance will fade,
Leaving traces of joy conveyed.
Yet in our hearts, their rhythm stays,
A memory of winter's playful ways.

Frost's Hidden Chorus

Beneath the surface, whispers arise,
Frost's hidden chorus sings to the skies.
Each crystal note, a story told,
Of winter's embrace, both fierce and bold.

Softly beneath the shrouded night,
Nature cradles the silence tight.
With every flake, the song unfolds,
In gentle tones, the warmth it holds.

Icicles hang like chimes that ring,
Dancing lightly on the breath of spring.
A symphony of cold and light,
Echoing softly through the night.

When the dawn breaks, the chorus fades,
Yet in the heart, the melody invades.
Remembered whispers bring delight,
Frost's hidden chorus, a sweet respite.

As seasons shift and time moves on,
We hold the echoes, though they're gone.
In the quiet, the music flows,
A reminder of what winter knows.

Whispers of Winter's Veil

A blanket of white drapes the earth,
Whispers of winter, a quiet rebirth.
Each snowflake falls with delicate grace,
Covering the world in a soft embrace.

The frosty air carries secrets old,
Stories of warmth through the bitter cold.
As shadows stretch in the fading light,
We gather close to the hearth tonight.

Echoes of laughter dance in the air,
Filling the night with love and care.
Through windows aglow, warmth spills out,
In winter's grasp, we laugh and shout.

Nature sleeps beneath the snow's soft fold,
While dreams unfold in the bitter cold.
With every whisper, the night reveals,
The tender magic of winter's veils.

So here we stand, hand in hand,
In the silence of a snowy land.
With every breath, we feel the thrill,
Of winter's whispers, eternal still.

Enchanted by the Chill

Whispers of frost dance in the air,
Leaves shimmer softly, stripped bare.
Moonlight glistens on frozen ground,
In this moment, magic is found.

A breath of ice, so crisp and bright,
Stars twinkle down, a wondrous sight.
Nature's hush, a tranquil song,
In this stillness, we belong.

Glistening branches, laden with white,
Invite the heart to dreams at night.
Each snowflake falls, a fleeting grace,
Painting the world with a soft embrace.

Through the silent woods we roam,
Wrapped in warmth, far from home.
With every step, a tale unfolds,
In the chill, the heart beholds.

The night deepens, shadows grow long,
In the frost, we hum a song.
Together in this enchanted scene,
Bound by the chill, we've never been.

The Hidden Life Beneath

Roots intertwine in the dark embrace,
Whispered secrets, a timeless place.
Life stirs gently, hidden away,
Nurtured in silence, come what may.

Fungi flourish, a vibrant hue,
Tiny worlds thrive, old and new.
In the shadows, life forms weave,
Threads of existence, none perceive.

A harmony hums in muted tones,
Subtle rhythms, earthy moans.
Unseen journeys, a mystic dance,
Woven together by chance.

Through ancient trails, the whispers flow,
Beneath the surface, life will grow.
In the soil, where wonders hide,
Nature's cycle, alive with pride.

In quietude, the secrets stay,
Tales of life, come what may.
In the shadows, beneath the core,
Lives intertwined forevermore.

Intriguing Shadows in White

Ghostly forms in the pale moonlight,
Whispers linger, soft and slight.
Each shadow dances, a fleeting trace,
In the night, they find their place.

Figures move, with secrets shared,
In the silence, hearts are bared.
A fleeting glimpse, a breathless sigh,
Beneath the stars, they softly lie.

Snowflakes fall, draped in mystery,
Creating tales of ancient history.
With every flake, a story spins,
In the echoes, where silence begins.

Underneath the spectral light,
Life and dreams blend in the night.
Figures shift, with whispers near,
In the shadows, we hold dear.

A world of whispers, soft and bright,
Intriguing shadows, veiled in white.
Through the night, they come and go,
In their dance, we find the glow.

The Veiled Harmony

In twilight's grasp, where shadows lay,
Melodies linger, gently sway.
A harmony veiled in twilight's hue,
Calls to the heart, both old and new.

Softly rising, a whispering breeze,
Carries echoes through the trees.
In the silence, secrets unfold,
Tales of the past, yet untold.

Moonlit paths where time does bend,
Every note a path to transcend.
Dancing lightly, the night birds sing,
A symphony born on fragile wing.

In this moment, the world stands still,
Wrapped in dreams with a gentle thrill.
The veiled harmony wraps around,
A sacred space where peace is found.

With each heartbeat, the music grows,
In the shadows, a story flows.
Through the night, in whispers divine,
Veiled in harmony, your hand in mine.

In the Stillness of Chill

In the morning light so pale,
Snowflakes dance like quiet mail.
Whispers soft in frosty air,
Nature holds its breath with care.

Trees stand cloaked in purest white,
Branches arching, capturing light.
Footsteps crunch on frozen ground,
In this peace, our hearts are found.

Clouds drift slowly, gray and low,
Time moves gently, soft and slow.
Moments linger, sweet and still,
In the hush of winter's thrill.

Skies fade into shades of blue,
Silence weaves its magic too.
Nature pauses, time a thrill,
In the stillness of chill, we feel.

Every breath a misty sigh,
A world where dreams refuse to die.
In twilight's glow, we find our way,
In the stillness, we wish to stay.

The Unseen Traces of Winter

Beneath the snow, the ground holds tight,
Life's whispers kept from winter's bite.
Frosted edges, sharp and bright,
In the dark, unseen delight.

Each step unveils a hidden trail,
Stories wrapped in icy veil.
Nature's secrets lie in wait,
A frozen kiss, a destined fate.

Silent shadows dance at dusk,
Promising warmth in the musk.
Winter's grip may seem so strong,
Yet beneath, the pulse goes on.

Rivers freeze but hearts remain,
Love flows freely, soft as rain.
Traces linger, gentle signs,
In the cold, our spirit shines.

We gather close, in fireside glow,
Sharing stories, letting go.
In winter's grasp, the world stands still,
Unseen traces our hearts fulfill.

Frozen Alchemy of Secrets

In the freeze, a secret stirs,
Molten dreams like silken furs.
Chill ignites the alchemist's spark,
Transforming shadows, brightening dark.

Snowflakes weave their tales untold,
Patterns intricate, soft yet bold.
Mirrored realms of frost and ice,
Nature's canvas, pure and nice.

Underneath the sparkling sheen,
Life awakens, quiet and keen.
Alchemy in every breath,
Whispers of life amid the death.

Gentle magic, soft as pearl,
In frigid air, a hidden whirl.
Turning cold into beauty's grace,
In this stillness, we find our place.

Frozen realms of heart and mind,
In the chill, true treasures find.
Secrets buried in crystal light,
Frozen alchemy, pure delight.

The Art of Frost

Frost paints stories on window panes,
Delicate layers, nature's gains.
A breath of winter added flair,
Whispered tales hang in the air.

Leaves turn silver, branches gleam,
Winter casts its frosty dream.
Crystal beauty, sharp and clear,
In every flake, a memory dear.

Each morn brings a fresh display,
Nature's art in a fleeting way.
Time moves on, yet here it stays,
In the magic of winter's gaze.

Frosted edges pick up light,
Creating wonders in the night.
The art of frost, a fleeting phase,
Captured moments in a haze.

Softly fades as seasons change,
But in our hearts, it feels so strange.
In every winter's gentle loss,
We learn to treasure the art of frost.

The Winter's Mysterious Dance

Whispers roam through the silent night,
Snowflakes twirl in the pale moonlight.
Branches sway with a graceful sway,
Nature holds breath as shadows play.

Shivering winds weave tales so deep,
In icy blankets, the world sleeps.
Footprints vanish, a fleeting trace,
The heart of winter, a timeless chase.

Stars above, in their chilly glow,
Guide the dance where the cold winds blow.
Magic swirls in the frosty air,
A silent wonder, beyond compare.

Frozen ponds hold a mirror so clear,
Reflecting dreams that disappear.
Beneath the surface, secrets lie,
In winter's grasp, we silently sigh.

As shadows deepen, the world stands still,
Moments linger, the heart to fill.
In every flake, a story hides,
In whispers soft, the winter bides.

Frosty Caresses

Gentle fingers brush the ground,
In soft silence, peace is found.
Layers of frost coat every leaf,
Nature wears its crystal brief.

Morning light through branches peeks,
Whispers of frost, the silence speaks.
A fragile world wrapped in white,
Joyful hearts bask in the light.

Pines stand tall, their arms outstretched,
Embracing winters, cold, beloved sketch.
A shiver dances upon the skin,
Embodying the joy within.

The air is crisp, the breath is seen,
In frosted fields, a life serene.
Every corner a new delight,
Wrapped snugly in the winter's bite.

Footsteps crunch on the powdery trail,
In this wonderland, dreams prevail.
With every step, stories unfold,
Of frosty caresses, quietly told.

The Stillness Beneath

Beneath the snow, silence brews,
Calmness wraps in gentle hues.
A world asleep, in white it lies,
Hidden whispers in icy sighs.

Branches bending under the weight,
Nature holds its breath, awaits.
Frosty crystals, a tangled lace,
Draping the earth in a soft embrace.

Dreams of spring sleep in the frost,
In winter's arms, not all is lost.
Life prepares in quiet grace,
Hidden depths, a sacred space.

Hushed and still, the moments flow,
Under the surface, life starts to grow.
Each breath of wind, a secret sent,
In winter's heart, our time is spent.

Time may pass; the seasons turn,
But in this stillness, we can learn.
To find the beauty in the freeze,
In empty spaces, nature's ease.

Silent Melodies of the Frost

Softly falls the winter's song,
In gentle notes, we all belong.
Frosted breezes play the tune,
Underneath the silver moon.

A quiet hush blankets the earth,
In every flake, a silent birth.
Crystalline laughter fills the air,
Echoing gently, sweet and rare.

Whispers drift like feathered sighs,
In hidden realms where magic lies.
In every breath, the melody glows,
Carried by winds where the stillness flows.

Trees stand tall in frosty grace,
Caressing the dreams that time can't erase.
Nature's symphony, wondrous and bright,
Plays on the heart in the stillness of night.

In winter's grasp, we find our song,
With silent melodies, we all belong.
Through every beat, the world aligns,
In harmony, as nature shines.

Chilling Confessions

In the quiet night, whispers grow,
Secrets tangled in the cold,
Shadows lengthen, stories unfold,
Courage falters, warmth feels slow.

Breath hangs heavy, clouds of white,
Eyes gaze deep into the dark,
Hearts confess what dreams ignite,
Fears laid bare leave their mark.

Snowflakes twirl like thoughts in flight,
Each one holds a tale unshared,
Frozen hopes in the pale moonlight,
Lonely hearts long to be paired.

Echoes of laughter, gone too soon,
Memories dance on frosty air,
Time retreating, like the moon,
Confessions drift without a care.

Underneath the stars, we freeze,
Moments creep like icy streams,
Chilling whispers in the breeze,
Our confessions, all like dreams.

Beneath the Blankets of Ice

Beneath the blankets, silence lies,
Whispers of winter play their tune,
Stars emerge in darkening skies,
As frost and shadows softly croon.

In the stillness, secrets stay,
Voices echo a muffled sound,
Frozen thoughts in disarray,
Lost in dreams, they swirl around.

Under icy layers, we wait,
Stories buried, deep and wide,
Held by time, we'll contemplate,
What truths in the cold we hide.

Shimmering frost like lace so fine,
Nature whispers, a gentle sigh,
Beneath the ice, our hearts align,
Where hopes and fears forever lie.

As the world sleeps, secrets keep,
Blankets cover both pain and grace,
In the silence, we find the deep,
Beneath the ice, we find our place.

Frosty Fables

Fables weave in the frosty air,
Tales of hearts, courageous and bold,
Legends spoken with a gentle care,
In the snow, where dreams unfold.

Once upon a time, it's told,
Wanderers brave, lost in the storm,
Their spirits warm, yet hearts grown cold,
In the white, they seek the norm.

Snowflakes drift like thoughts of old,
Each one tells of passion and pain,
Through the night, their stories hold,
Whispers linger, like sweet refrain.

Frozen dreams in a world so vast,
Every breath, a fable large,
Threads of time, through winters passed,
In the chill, we make our charge.

As the fables bend and sway,
Through frost and flame, we find our light,
In every tale, there's always a way,
To tell our truth beneath the night.

Echoes in the Frozen Air

Echoes whisper in frozen air,
Memories glide like soft snowflakes,
Hidden feelings, secrets laid bare,
In the stillness, the heart aches.

Voices linger, long after dusk,
Tales of love, loss, and despair,
Among the shadows, a fragile husk,
Each breath held within the glare.

In the chill, we find our place,
Cold like ice, yet warm with dreams,
Reflections dance, a ghostly grace,
In the silence, nothing seems.

Carried forth by winter's breath,
Echoes of what once was whole,
Past and future blend in depth,
Within the frost, lies the soul.

So let the echoes softly sing,
Of moments lost and found anew,
In the frozen air, our hearts take wing,
Flying forth to a brighter hue.

Whispers Unseen

In shadows soft, the whispers flow,
They dance like leaves in gentle woe.
A murmur here, a sigh at night,
Tales of dreams drift out of sight.

The wind will carry secrets near,
In twilight's hush, the heart will hear.
Mysteries wrapped in silence tight,
Echoes linger, shadows light.

Through hidden paths where silence dwells,
The world unfurls its quiet spells.
Each secret shared in twilight's grace,
A fleeting touch, a soft embrace.

When night deepens and stars arise,
Whispers weave through the velvet skies.
Underneath the moon's soft glow,
Untold stories gently flow.

So pause awhile, in evening's tune,
Let whispers guide beneath the moon.
For in the dark, we find the key,
To mysteries that set us free.

Secrets in the Moonlit Snow

Footprints fade in the silvery glow,
A canvas white, where dreams can grow.
Each flake a secret, softly spun,
Beneath the gaze of the silent sun.

In drifts of white, the whispers hide,
Tales of the night where shadows bide.
The stillness wraps the world so tight,
Cradling secrets till morning light.

Snowflakes twirl with a graceful sound,
Messages lost on frosty ground.
With every step so light and slow,
A journey through the moonlit snow.

The chill becomes a gentle sigh,
As dreams awaken in winter's eye.
Each glimmer holds a tale untold,
In silver silence, secrets bold.

As dawn approaches, the magic fades,
Yet in our hearts, the memory stays.
For hidden joints, where wishes flow,
Remain in us, like the moonlit snow.

The Cold's Gentle Poetry

In frosted breath, the world awakes,
Each crystal shard, a memory makes.
A playful breeze with stories to tell,
Of winter's charm and its icy spell.

The chill weaves softly through the trees,
A tender touch, a whispered freeze.
Beneath the frost, life sleeps so sound,
In stillness deep, while dreams abound.

In every flake that tumbles down,
A snapshot of nature's fragile crown.
Each icy breath, a verse so sweet,
The cold writes poetry at our feet.

The quiet nights and distant stars,
Hold secrets close in velvet bars.
With every breath, the world awaits,
The cold's soft touch, the heart sedates.

As dawn unfolds, the colors rise,
The gentle poetry, a sweet surprise.
Embrace the chill, let it inspire,
For in the cold lives heart's desire.

Beneath the Shimmering Light

Stars like pearls in a velvet sea,
Whisper softly, come dance with me.
A tapestry of dreams unfurls,
As night reveals its jeweled pearls.

Each fleck of light, a tale to share,
Promises hidden in moonlit air.
Beneath the shimmer, hearts ignite,
Lost in wonder, lost in night.

In shadows deep, the magic grows,
As nature's beauty softly shows.
With every twinkle, hope takes flight,
In the embrace of the shimmering light.

Hold close the dreams that spark and shine,
For every star is truly divine.
Together we'll weave a story bright,
Forever bound beneath the night.

So let the cosmos gently weave,
A dance of light for us to believe.
For beneath the stars, love finds its rite,
And hearts are warmed in the shimmering light.

Illuminated by Winter's Touch

The frost bites softly at the dawn,
A glimmering veil on the frozen lawn.
Trees stand tall with branches bare,
Whispers of silence linger in the air.

Crystals sparkle under the pale sun,
Each flake a story, a journey begun.
Pine trees cloaked in blankets of white,
Hold secrets hidden in the quiet light.

Footsteps crunch on the icy ground,
A serenade of winter, a soft surround.
The world transformed, a magical scene,
Where the heart finds solace, calm, and serene.

As evening falls, the colors fade,
Stars emerge, in darkness they're laid.
A dance of shadows on the snow,
In winter's embrace, we let our hearts flow.

Warmth from within lights our souls,
In winter's grip, we become whole.
Illuminated under the wintry glow,
A timeless beauty lay wrapped below.

Fractal Patterns in the Cold

Patterns emerge in the blanket of white,
Fractal designs dancing in the night.
Nature's artwork, so vivid and bright,
Each flake a marvel, pure and slight.

Whorls and spirals converge on the ground,
Silent music, a magical sound.
Branches glisten with icy lace,
In this frozen, intricate space.

A breath of winter hangs in the air,
A fleeting moment, ethereal and rare.
Kaleidoscopes of beauty unfold,
As stories of winter are silently told.

Let the snowflakes dance as they fall,
Creating beauty, enchanting us all.
In the chill of night, they wriggle and weave,
Fractal patterns, we dare to believe.

With each twist and turn, a tale untold,
In stark silhouettes, images unfold.
Winter's canvas, a breath of the old,
Fractal patterns, in the cold.

Frost-Kissed Whispers

Frost-kissed whispers greet the dawn,
Nature sighs, as the day is drawn.
Each blade of grass, a sparkling gem,
In the world being painted, we stem.

Whispers float on the chilled breeze,
Carrying secrets among the trees.
Buds may wait for the warmth of spring,
But the hush of winter has its own zing.

Crimson sunsets cloak the horizon,
As shadows stretch and night comes on.
Underneath the tranquil sky,
Frost-kissed whispers gently sigh.

The world at peace, a soft retreat,
Where the heart's quick rhythm finds its beat.
Each moment savored, a precious find,
In the art of winter, we unwind.

The frost that clings, a delicate lace,
Renews our spirits in its embrace.
With every heartbeat, whisper and clutch,
We revel in winter's frost-kissed touch.

The Quiet Flurries

The quiet flurries start to dance,
In the hush of winter, a fleeting glance.
Snowflakes swirl, a gentle ballet,
As nature rests in white array.

Softly they land on the silent ground,
Tales from the clouds, they swirl around.
Each drift a magic, a story untold,
In whispers of winter, brave and bold.

Streetlamps glow with a golden hue,
Casting shadows in the evening's dew.
The world adorned in shimmering light,
As the quiet flurries paint the night.

In the stillness, we find our space,
Moments that linger, a warm embrace.
With every flake, so soft and sweet,
The quiet flurries, our hearts they greet.

So let us wander in this serene scene,
Wrapped in dreams, where we've always been.
With winter's breath all around,
The quiet flurries, peace we've found.

Frozen Soliloquy

In silence wrapped, the world asleep,
A whispering wind begins to creep.
Nature holds its breath in peace,
As time, in frosted stillness, cease.

Each flake a thought, a fleeting trace,
Soft memories of a warm embrace.
Icicles hang like frozen tears,
Marking the passage of fleeting years.

Reflections dance on glassy streams,
Mirrored dreams in winter's schemes.
A breath of frost, a moment's pause,
Captures the heart with quiet cause.

Underneath the vast, cold sky,
The spirit soars, the soul waves bye.
In solitude, my heart, it knows,
This frozen path, a life exposed.

But in this chill, I find my fire,
A flicker deep, a pure desire.
To break the ice, to feel the sun,
In frozen thoughts, I find I'm one.

A Chill in the Airwaves

Through valleys deep, the whispers glide,
Carried by the breath of the tide.
A chill descends, the silence hums,
As winter's melody softly drums.

Crystals form on frozen lakes,
Nature's voice in stillness wakes.
Every sigh, a crystal note,
In the chill, my heart, it floats.

The air is thick with tales untold,
Of ancient times and joys of old.
Ghosts of warmth in shadows play,
As sunlight dims and fades away.

A fleeting touch of icy grace,
Each breeze, a soft and tender space.
In every breath, the world aligns,
With winter's song, forever finds.

So listen close, let silence grow,
In winter's grasp, the heart shall know.
Each chilly wave, a gentle cue,
To navigate the path so true.

Enigma of the Winter Sky

Beneath the dome of endless blue,
Stars shimmer soft, a timeless hue.
The moon hangs low, a silver sigh,
In the enigma of the winter sky.

Clouds drift slow, like secrets shared,
Moonlit dances, all prepared.
In twilight's breath, a story spun,
Of frosted nights and days undone.

Comets trail with whispered dreams,
Silent echoes in starlit streams.
Each moment wrapped in cold repose,
The universe, the heart, it knows.

Frosted branches, a fragile lace,
Reflect the light with quiet grace.
In winter's arms, the soul shall thrive,
As long-lost hopes begin to strive.

In every gaze at the vast expanse,
The mysteries of life enhance.
In the chill, I sense the flow,
Of endless paths that twist and grow.

Beneath the White Embrace

Blanketed deep in gentle white,
Nature's hush, a pure delight.
Each flake a kiss, a soft caress,
In winter's arms, I find my rest.

Trees stand tall, adorned in lace,
Guardians of this tranquil space.
A pathway winds through woods so still,
Beneath the peace, the heart can fill.

Birds seek refuge, a cozy nest,
In quiet corners, they find rest.
Every rustle, a story unfolds,
In the embrace of winter's hold.

The world transformed in pristine charm,
A calming touch, a soothing balm.
Underneath this frosty light,
I find my strength to face the night.

So let the snow fall soft and gray,
For in its dance, I find my way.
Beneath the white, the heart can soar,
In winter's grace, I am reborn.

Gentle Whispers of the Cold

The wind hums low, a soothing sound,
Crystals twirl, gently dance around.
Branches sigh with a silver hue,
Nature's breath whispers soft and true.

Stars blink bright in the frosty night,
Moonlight bathes the world in white.
Each snowflake falls, a fleeting thought,
Warmth in hearts, no battles fought.

Silent roads leading far away,
Footprints trace where we used to play.
Veils of frost caress the dawn,
In gentle peace, the worries gone.

Breezes glide like secrets shared,
Every moment, tenderly cared.
Rustling leaves, the trees hold tight,
A lullaby sung in the quiet night.

The world transformed with soft embrace,
Nature wraps us in its grace.
Whispers fading with morning light,
Leaving dreams until next night.

Masquerade of the Ice Queen

In a realm where shadows gleam,
A queen weaves her frosty dream.
With shimmering lace and icy crown,
She dances gracefully, never to frown.

Glistening halls echo her name,
Each step a note in a crystal game.
Masks of snowflakes flutter by,
Mysteries wrapped in the night sky.

Her laughter sparkles like frozen streams,
Kisses bestowed with winter's gleams.
Adorned in jewels, the stars align,
In her court, the world feels divine.

Glacial winds carry her song,
A tale of ice where hearts belong.
Whirling skirts, a flurry of grace,
In her presence, time finds its place.

As midnight falls, the show unfolds,
Stories of love and courage told.
With each twirl, a secret spun,
In the masquerade, winter's fun.

With a sigh, she bids adieu,
Leaving behind a world anew.
Echoes linger where she had been,
In the heart of ice, the warmth unseen.

Veins of Winter's Heart

Deep in the woods, the silence grows,
Frosted branches in soft repose.
Nature's pulse beats slow and clear,
In the stillness, winter draws near.

Under the snow, life waits concealed,
The earth's embrace, a secret shield.
Veins of chill run through the night,
Awakening dreams of spring's delight.

Frozen streams whisper to the moon,
A lullaby, a tender tune.
Crystals sparkle on the ground,
Nature's pulse, a soothing sound.

Stars appear like scattered pearls,
Winds weave stories, dance and twirls.
Every crystal, a tale unknown,
Within the frost, the seeds are sown.

The heart of winter beats so bold,
In icy grip, nature unfolds.
A flicker of warmth, a hint of light,
Veins of winter, a beautiful sight.

As dawn breaks, the chill retreats,
In every breath, the world competes.
But in the shadows, moments saved,
The essence of winter, softly engraved.

Echoing Lullabies of the Frost

In the hush of the evening's glow,
Frosty whispers begin to flow.
Lullabies from the moonlit skies,
A serenade where peace lies.

Crickets sing in a frozen choir,
Nature hums with a secret desire.
Each note drifts on the chilling breeze,
Carried softly among the trees.

Dreams wrapped in the softest snow,
Muffled voices, sweet and low.
Guided by the silver light,
In winter's arms, we feel so right.

Every sigh, a promise made,
In the shadows, lovers wade.
Hands entwined 'neath the starlit cloak,
Sharing tales that were never spoke.

As frost weaves patterns on the ground,
Soft echoes of laughter abound.
The night's embrace, a gentle call,
In this serene space, we feel it all.

With each heartbeat, the earth awakes,
Nature stirs, and the winter breaks.
But till first light, let laughter soar,
In echoing lullabies, forevermore.

Whispers from Icebound Dreams

In the quiet of night,
Whispers dance like phantoms,
Frosted tales stir in sleep,
Under the silver moon.

Lost in a world of white,
Echoes of dreams take flight,
Each breath hangs in the air,
A soft sigh in silence.

Glistening eyes catch stars,
Frozen worlds softly gleam,
The past wrapped in winter,
Memories held in ice.

Gentle winds carry hopes,
As shadows weave through trees,
A tapestry of frost,
Crafted by fleeting dreams.

In the stillness we find,
Secrets of heart and mind,
Whispers linger and fade,
In the chill of the night.

Frostbound Whispers

Beneath the blanket white,
Whispers softly emerge,
Crisp tales of the still night,
In frostbound, tender hush.

With every icy breath,
A story gently told,
In the shimmer of stars,
Where time seems to unfold.

Frost grips the silent earth,
Hopes are sealed in a dream,
Stars twinkle in the deep,
In the magic of gleam.

Echoes ride the cool wind,
Through branches dipped in frost,
Nature's quiet secrets,
In the night, never lost.

Underneath silver skies,
Life pauses to reflect,
In a world spun of ice,
Whispers sharpened and perfect.

The Silence of Snowflakes

Snowflakes softly glide down,
In their dance, time stands still,
Each one holds a secret,
In the quiet, a thrill.

Blanketing the cold ground,
Whispers merge with the night,
The world wrapped in silence,
A vision pure and bright.

Falling soft from above,
Kissing earth's frozen brow,
So gently they embrace,
Nature's moment, here now.

Snow drifts cradle the dark,
As stars blanket the sky,
Each flake a fleeting thought,
That whispers and floats by.

In the still of the world,
Life's echoes cease to be,
Wrapped in the hush of snow,
We find tranquility.

Echoes of a Frigid Dream

In the heart of the chill,
Dreams linger like shadows,
Echoes of what once was,
Beneath the frost-laden bows.

A symphony of stillness,
Where the whispers of ice
Travel far in the night,
Binding time, paying price.

As snow trails weave and spin,
Stories drift on the breeze,
Leaves a mark on the ground,
Frozen words among trees.

Frigid thoughts lost in space,
The dance of winter's kiss,
In quietude and peace,
Moments gather in bliss.

With the dawn comes a glow,
Yet the cold holds its sway,
In echoes of dreams past,
The whispers still will play.

Melodies of the Icebound World

Whispers echo through the trees,
Where frost and silence weave with ease.
The chilling breeze plays softly near,
Creating songs only hearts can hear.

Glistening flakes fall from the sky,
Dancing gently, as they drift by.
In the stillness, a symphony,
The icebound world sings joyfully.

Each step cracks the dormant ice,
Nature's voice, both cold and nice.
Footprints follow a winding trail,
Leading where the echoes sail.

In the distance, shadows play,
As the sun begins to sway.
Colors shimmer, twinkling bright,
In the heart of winter's night.

From frosty lakes to mountains high,
Magic fills the open sky.
In this world, we find our way,
Where melodies of peace hold sway.

Veils of Crystal

Glistening curtains drape the trees,
Enchanted whispers float on the breeze.
The world adorned in shimmering white,
Beneath the soft, caressing light.

Each branch is dressed in diamond lace,
Nature's touch, an elegant grace.
A realm where dreams and frost combine,
Veils of crystal, pure and divine.

Footsteps leave their fleeting marks,
Tracing paths through frozen parks.
Where beauty lies in every flake,
A tranquil heart for winter's sake.

As shadows stretch with day's retreat,
Peace surrounds in softest heat.
The veil, a promise rich and deep,
In crystal hush, the world will sleep.

Here in this serene tableau,
Silent whispers tell us so.
Revel in the stillness grand,
Veils of crystal, sweet and planned.

The Frost-kissed Passage

A winding trail through dusk's embrace,
Where frost-kissed paths find their place.
In silver gloss, the world unfolds,
Secrets whispered, courage bold.

Each breath a cloud in icy air,
Wonder lingers everywhere.
Frosty fingers trace the ground,
In this chilled passage, we are found.

Winds weave tales of ancient lore,
While the night unveils her core.
Stars peek through the frosted veil,
Guiding hearts where dreams derail.

Among the pines, an echo sings,
Of joy that winter surely brings.
With every step, the magic grows,
In this passage, life bestows.

Beneath the moon's soft silver light,
Shadows dance, a charming sight.
Through the frost-kissed passage wide,
We walk together, heart and guide.

Secrets in the White Drift

In the stillness of a crystal night,
Secrets glow in ghostly light.
Beneath the blanket, soft and deep,
Nature's whispers dare to sleep.

Each flake that falls carries a tale,
Of journeys lost and paths unveiled.
The silent grip of winter's hold,
Cradles dreams, both new and old.

Wandering through the depths of snow,
Every step, a chance to know.
The treasure buried, hidden tight,
Awaits the brave who seek the light.

Amidst the drifts, the secrets dwell,
In frosty air, they weave a spell.
An invitation, soft and sweet,
To find what makes the heart complete.

As dawn breaks with a gentle glow,
The world is kissed by melting snow.
In each moment, magic spins,
Secrets echo as the day begins.

Midnight's Whisper

In shadows deep, the silence speaks,
Stars twinkle bright, as daylight peaks.
A gentle breeze through branches sways,
Embracing dreams in night's soft haze.

The moonlight dances on the ground,
Whispers of secrets all around.
Each fleeting moment holds a spark,
In the stillness, life leaves its mark.

Voices of dreams in midnight's song,
A melody where we belong.
Each heartbeat syncs with twilight's sigh,
Under the vast and endless sky.

Time drifts slowly, shadows blend,
Every story finds its end.
Yet in the night, new tales unfold,
In whispers soft, both brave and bold.

As dawn approaches, silence fades,
But night's embrace forever stays.
In every twilight, a promise kept,
In midnight's whisper, dreams adept.

Secrets Within the Frosted Veil

Winter's breath on windows gleams,
Crystalline whispers weave through dreams.
Beneath the frost, the earth does sigh,
Holding secrets where shadows lie.

Branches bare in silver lace,
Nature's art, a ghostly grace.
Softly falling, snowflakes twirl,
Each a story, a hidden whirl.

Footsteps muffled, silence reigns,
Echoes of stories in icy chains.
Buried wishes in frozen time,
Awakened softly, a whispered rhyme.

Nature's secrets, quietly penned,
In every corner, where moments blend.
The world transformed, a white retreat,
Guarding wonders, both bitter and sweet.

As winter wanes, truths shall break,
A gentle thaw, the earth will wake.
Yet in the frost, reminders stay,
Of secrets held in a cold ballet.

The Language of Winter

The world in white, a hushed delight,
Whispers of frost, in day and night.
Every flake, a tale untold,
In silence strong, the brave and bold.

Crimson berries cling to life,
Against the cold, they end the strife.
Nature speaks in muted tones,
In winter's chill, we find our bones.

Pine trees stand in stoic grace,
Guardians of this frozen place.
With every wind that sweeps the land,
A language formed, both soft and grand.

The crackle of ice beneath the weight,
Echoes of time, a sacred fate.
Beneath the chill, the heart beats strong,
In winter's arms, we all belong.

As seasons change, the language flows,
In every storm, and in each snow.
From winter's depths, a warmth will rise,
In nature's heart, where love defies.

Soft Echoes of Frozen Whispers

Beneath the stars, a stillness grows,
In every breath, a secret flows.
Frosted whispers call the night,
In gentle tones, they bring delight.

Moonlit paths weave tales in white,
Leading souls to dance with light.
Every shadow holds a trace,
Of bygone days, a fleeting grace.

Frozen lakes mirror dreams of old,
Stories captured, waiting to unfold.
In every ripple, echoes ring,
Of winter's heart and what it brings.

As dawn approaches, whispers sway,
In morning glow, they drift away.
Yet in our hearts, they softly stay,
Guiding us gently, day by day.

In winter's realm, the echoes dwell,
Guardians of time, with tales to tell.
Softly whispered on icy breath,
Life's fragile dance, defying death.

Whispers of Ice Crystals

Delicate dancers in the night,
Twinkling softly, pure and bright.
Every shimmer tells a tale,
Of winter's breath and frosty veil.

They cling to branches, glimmering fair,
A fleeting moment, caught in air.
Each crystal unique, a fragile song,
In the silence where they belong.

Their whispers carry on the breeze,
A secret hush among the trees.
Nature's jewels, fragile and rare,
In winter's grip, a timeless flair.

As dawn breaks soft with muted hue,
The icy whispers bid adieu.
Yet in their glint, a memory stays,
A dance of light on chillier days.

Through every frost that we behold,
These ice crystals, stories told.
In winter's heart, they find their place,
A fleeting glimpse of frozen grace.

Hushed Footprints in the Snow

A trail of silence marks the ground,
In pure white blankets, peace is found.
Each step a story left behind,
Of wanderers lost in the mind.

In twilight's glow, they softly gleam,
A whispered path, a secret dream.
With every crunch beneath the foot,
A moment captured, solitude.

The cold air breathes, a shared delight,
Footprints fading into night.
Beneath the stars, they slowly wane,
Leaving memories etched in the grain.

Who walked this path, with heart so light?
What tales were shared on a wintry night?
Each imprint tells of journeys past,
Fragrant whispers, shadows cast.

And when the dawn breaks, bright and clear,
New footprints mark the coming year.
In nature's dance, the cycle flows,
Back to silence, where stillness grows.

Silent Stories Beneath the Surface

Under snow and ice, secrets sleep,
In a hushed world, still and deep.
Where whispers weave through frozen streams,
And nature cradles broken dreams.

Beneath the frost, life waits and hides,
In silence, where the mystery bides.
Like pages turned in ancient books,
Each hidden layer gently crooks.

Crystals form on the ground so bare,
Waiting for spring to break the air.
They hold the echoes of seasons gone,
In their embrace, life goes on.

What stories dwell beneath the ice?
A timeless dance, a game of dice.
In quietude, they softly tread,
The beats of life, a path well led.

As winter yields to the warming sun,
The silent stories come undone.
Revealed at last, a vibrant hue,
In spring's embrace, life greets anew.

The Enigma of Winter's Breath

A chilling sigh through trees does weave,
In winter's clutch, we can believe.
Each gust a riddle, crisp and clear,
Binding the world in silver sheer.

What secrets lie in breath so cold?
Stories of frost, of legends old.
In every whisper, magic swirls,
The dance of snowflakes, twirls and twirls.

Across the landscape, shadows cast,
The enigma of the season vast.
With every pause, with every sigh,
The world transforms, as time slips by.

Reflective stillness in the air,
A mystery held with utmost care.
What lies beneath the snowy shroud?
The heart of winter, soft and proud.

As the sun dips low in the sky,
Winter's breath whispers its goodbye.
But the enigma, though it fades,
Leaves traces of joy in frozen glades.

Shimmering Silence

In the hush of night time,
Stars begin their gentle glow,
Quiet dreams take flight,
While the moon casts a shadow.

Shimmering Silence

Trees stand tall and still,
Wrapped in silver light,
Nature's breath is soft,
Cradling the tranquil night.

Shimmering Silence

Footsteps fade on the ground,
Echoing through the air,
In this peaceful embrace,
Sorrow finds no care.

Shimmering Silence

Moments linger like dew,
Catching dreams as they fall,
In the shimmering silence,
Whispers echo through all.

Shimmering Silence

Hearts align with the stars,
A melody so sweet,
In the darkness we're free,
Finding solace so fleet.

Shimmering Silence

Within this sacred time,
The world feels vast and wide,
In shimmering silence,
We hold the night with pride.

Frosted Whispers

Breeze dances through the trees,
Carrying secrets untold,
Frosted whispers glide,
In the winter's bold cold.

Frosted Whispers

Each flake a tiny song,
Crafted in nature's hands,
As the sunlight breaks through,
Painting soft white lands.

Frosted Whispers

Silent footsteps echo,
Amidst the winter's cheer,
Tales of warmth and light,
Banter softly appear.

Frosted Whispers

Eyes wide with wonder,
As the world shines anew,
The frost kisses the ground,
A canvas wrapped in blue.

Frosted Whispers

In this serene moment,
Nature whispers so low,
Frosted whispers linger,
In a timeless glow.

Frosted Whispers

Under the crystal sky,
Where dreams and wishes play,
Frosted whispers unite,
Leading hearts on their way.

Beneath the Frosty Blanket

Fields lie dressed in white,
A serene slumber reigns,
Beneath the frosty blanket,
Winter softly remains.

Beneath the Frosty Blanket

Nature takes a deep breath,
Hibernation begins,
Trees trimmed with icy lace,
As the stillness spins.

Beneath the Frosty Blanket

Hidden beneath the chill,
Life softly breathes below,
Awaiting spring's gentle kiss,
To melt the winter's snow.

Beneath the Frosty Blanket

In this frozen moment,
Dreams await their time,
To awaken lush and green,
To dance in daylight's shine.

Beneath the Frosty Blanket

But for now, it's quiet,
A world of silver hues,
Beneath the frosty blanket,
Dreams still hold their views.

Beneath the Frosty Blanket

A quiet harmony wraps,
As stars twinkle bright,
Beneath the frosty blanket,
The canvas of the night.

Enigma of the White Drift

In the depth of the forest,
A veil of snow conceals,
Whispers of the unknown,
A secret that it reveals.

Enigma of the White Drift

Each drift tells a story,
Of journeys left untold,
Where the earth meets the sky,
In spirals of pure gold.

Enigma of the White Drift

Footprints lost to the past,
In the shimmer of frost,
Every breath of the chill,
Tells of moments we've lost.

Enigma of the White Drift

Yet beauty lies in silence,
Within this snowy maze,
An enigma of pure wonder,
Where the heart forever stays.

Enigma of the White Drift

As night wraps its cloak tight,
And stars come out to play,
The enigma of the white drift,
Calls the dreamers to stay.

Enigma of the White Drift

In this realm of stillness,
Time seems to stand still,
The enigma of the white drift,
Sings to the winter chill.

Glimmers in the Flurry

Snowflakes dance in quiet air,
A fleeting touch, both light and rare.
Underneath the pale moon's glow,
Whispers of winter softly flow.

Stars emerge as shadows fade,
Magic weaves through every glade.
Nature's brush, a canvas white,
Painting dreams in soft twilight.

Branches wear a glistening crown,
Hushed serenity comes down.
Sparkling trails where footsteps lie,
In this world, all spirits fly.

Echoes of laughter, rapture's call,
In the flurry, we rise and fall.
Hope like embers in the night,
Guides us through till morning light.

Glimmers fade, yet memories stay,
Winter's breath will fade away.
Yet in hearts, the warmth persists,
In glowing dreams, we still exist.

Breath of the Winter Ghosts

In the hush, a chill descends,
Echoes of laughter, where it ends.
Whispers of lost tales arise,
In twilight's glow and frosted skies.

Silhouettes in fields of white,
Ghostly figures in the night.
They dance upon the frozen ground,
In silence, secrets lost are found.

Softly drifting through the trees,
Carried on the frigid breeze.
The breath of ghosts, so faintly heard,
A chilling tale without a word.

Frosted windows, shadows play,
Memories linger, drift away.
Heartbeats echo in the cold,
Whispers of warmth in stories told.

As stars twinkle, time will teach,
Embrace the love that winter's reach.
For in the dark, we find our light,
In winter's breath, we hold on tight.

Frosty Footprints

Footprints etched in glistening snow,
Stories whisper where few will go.
Each step marks a fleeting tale,
In winter's heart, we set our sail.

Crystals form where the path leads,
Nature's canvas, pure thoughts and deeds.
With every step, the chill unfolds,
Secrets linger, warmth it holds.

Tracing lines through silver haze,
Echoes of laughter through cold days.
Winds carry melodies of cheer,
In frosty breath, the world feels near.

But as the sun begins to rise,
Footprints fade beneath the skies.
Yet in our hearts, they softly stay,
Memories warm in life's ballet.

With every flake that tumbles down,
New journeys form, where old ones drown.
In frosty footprints, paths anew,
Winter's tale we journey through.

The Lullaby of Ice

In the stillness, peace descends,
The lullaby where silence bends.
Crystalline beauty, soft and bright,
Wrapped in the arms of quiet night.

Melodies weave in the silver light,
The world asleep, in dreams so bright.
Pulsing whispers softly glide,
On frozen lakes, the stars abide.

Gentle sighs in the chilly air,
Nurtured hopes hang everywhere.
With each note, the cold rebirths,
In lullabies of frozen earth.

Feel the frost kiss your skin,
Dance with joy, let dreams begin.
In winter's grasp, we find our grace,
Time slows down in this sacred space.

As dawn awakes with blush and hue,
The lullaby whispers sweet and true.
Hold the night in your embrace,
For in its magic, we find our place.